AMERICA'S
10 Greatest
BATTLES

John Perritano

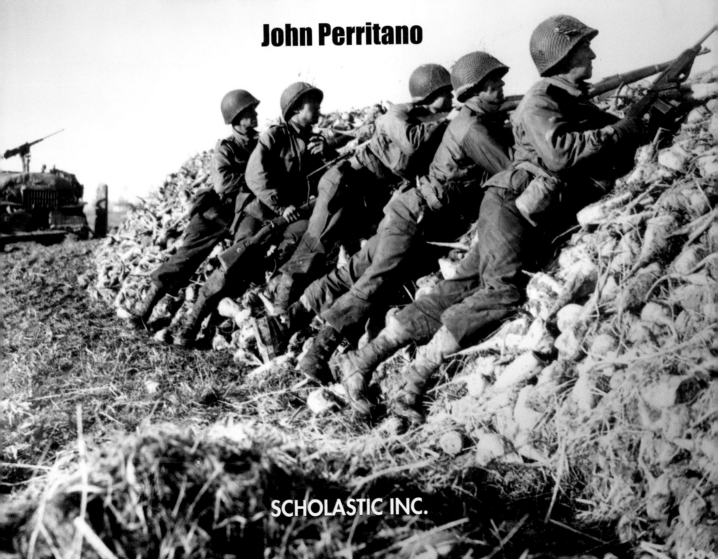

SCHOLASTIC INC.

Created by Q2A Bill Smith

ISBN 978-0-545-48723-8

12 11 10 9 8 7 6 5 4 3 2 1   13 14 15 16 17 18/0

Printed in the U.S.A.   40

First Scholastic printing, January 2013

Editor Jessica Cohn
Project Manager Shekhar Kapur
Art Director Joita Das
Designers Manish Kumar and Souvik Mukherjee
Picture Researcher Ranjana Batra

Contents

Power of War

American soldiers have fought in many battles, including the Battle of Long Island during the American Revolution.

"It is well that war is so terrible, or we should grow too fond of it."

When Confederate General Robert E. Lee uttered those words in 1862, the United States was mired in a bloody civil war that would claim more than 600,000 American lives. Wars are indeed terrible, as Lee observed, and their impact on history has been monumental.

Timeline of American Wars

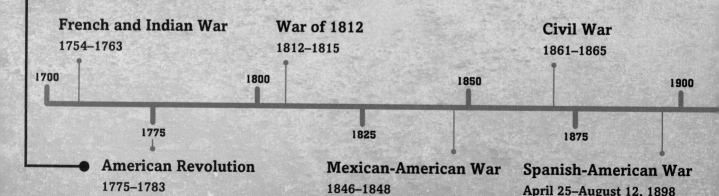

French and Indian War
1754–1763

War of 1812
1812–1815

Civil War
1861–1865

1700

1800

1850

1900

1775

1825

1875

American Revolution
1775–1783

Mexican-American War
1846–1848

Spanish-American War
April 25–August 12, 1898

Reasons to Fight

Americans have often gone to war for noble ideals. The Civil War was fought to preserve the Union. The U.S. joined World War I, in the words of President Woodrow Wilson, to make the world "safe for democracy." The U.S. entered World War II to rid the world of **fascism**.

Nation at War

Since its birth in 1776, the United States has fought in 12 major wars and numerous other conflicts. Some wars, such as the Persian Gulf War, lasted only a few months. Others, such as the Vietnam War, went on for many years. In each conflict, significant battles marked key turning points. Read on to better understand ten of the most pivotal U.S. battles and how they have affected our country and our lives.

U.S. warplanes dominated the skies in the Pacific during World War II.

The Battle Rages

What's the difference between a war and a battle? Wars are organized conflicts, generally between nations, in which each side tries to defeat its enemy. Battles are individual encounters between armies.

Just the Facts

The war in Afghanistan, which began in 2001, is now the longest war in U.S. history.

World War I 1914–1918	**Korean War** 1950–1953	**Persian Gulf War** August 1990–April 1991	**Iraq War** 2003–2011
1925		1975	2025
	1950		2000
World War II 1939–1945	**Vietnam War** 1964–1975	**War in Afghanistan** October 7, 2001–present	

Battle of Fort Duquesne ①

In the 1600s, European settlers began arriving in North America. Spain, France, Great Britain, and other European nations claimed portions of the continent for themselves. Their disputes over land led to numerous conflicts.

Battle Lines

Conflict
French and Indian War (1754–1763)

Dates of Battle
September and November 1758

Principal Commander
General John Forbes

In 1754, the British attempted to capture Fort Duquesne from the French. The fort was located in what is today Pittsburgh, Pennsylvania. It was built in a strategic position, where the Allegheny and Monongahela Rivers join to form the Ohio River.

While an officer in the Virginia militia, George Washington surrendered Fort Necessity after one of the first battles of the French and Indian War.

Washington Surrenders

Serving among the British forces was George Washington, a young man in charge of troops from the colony of Virginia. In preparation for battle, Washington and his men built a crude defensive structure they named Fort Necessity. But the French soon surrounded them, forcing Washington to surrender for the first and only time of his military career.

In the clashes that followed, several Native American groups helped the French, and the war became known as the French and Indian War. For the first three years, the French dominated. Then, late in 1758, British fortunes changed. In September, the British tried again to capture Fort Duquesne and force the French from the region.

Change in Fortunes

Once more, Washington was in charge of British forces from Virginia. On September 14, the British, under General John Forbes, sustained heavy casualties. In response, the British commanders decided to wait until spring before launching an assault. Washington disagreed. He did not want the French to have time to **reinforce** the garrison.

Washington learned that the Indian **allies** of the French had left, leaving the fort poorly defended. He ordered an attack. Knowing the odds were against them, the French escaped, after setting fire to their fort so that the British could not claim it. This was a turning point in the war, because the French later were pushed out of the Ohio Valley. Afterward, the British built a new fortress, called Fort Pitt. Washington, a natural leader, went on to become the first president of the United States.

This map shows the areas in North America dominated by Great Britain, France, and Spain at the time of the French and Indian War (1754–1763).

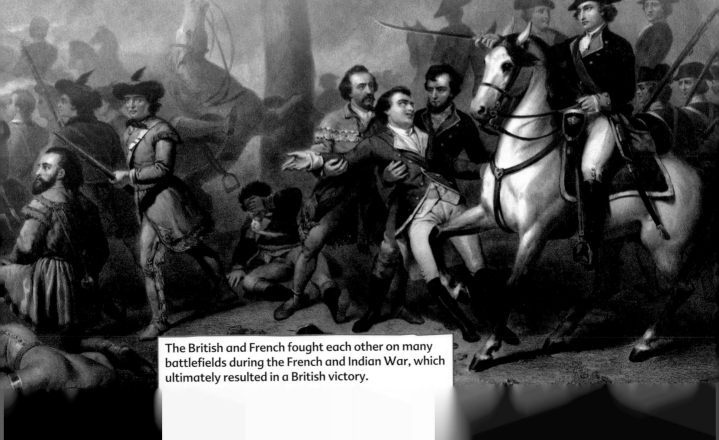

The British and French fought each other on many battlefields during the French and Indian War, which ultimately resulted in a British victory.

Battle of Saratoga ②

The United States was only a year old in 1777, and things were not going well for the Americans.

The British had won almost every major battle since the first shots were fired at the Battles of Lexington and Concord. Without help from France (Great Britain's archenemy), the American army and the revolution would be doomed.

Crush the Rebellion

In the fall of 1777, British General John Burgoyne tried to crush the American rebellion. He wanted to cut off New England from the rest of the country. Burgoyne planned to march south from Canada toward Albany, New York, as another British force, under General William Howe, advanced up the Hudson River from New York City. A third British army, commanded by Barry St. Leger, was to move east across central New York.

Things did not go as planned. On his way south, Burgoyne lost almost 1,000 troops that detoured to Vermont in search of supplies. In New York, the Americans blocked the British from moving east at Fort Stanwix. As for General Howe, he decided to march south to Philadelphia instead.

Battle Lines

Conflict
American Revolution (1775–1783)

Dates of Battle
September 19–October 7, 1777

Principal American Commander
General Horatio Gates

British General John Burgoyne surrendered after the British defeat at Saratoga. The loss prevented the British from dividing New England, birthplace of the American Revolution, from the rest of the colonies.

Benedict Arnold

Benedict Arnold is best remembered for being a traitor to America. Yet, the same Benedict Arnold was a hero during the Battle of Saratoga. On October 17, about 200 British troops pulled back to a defensive position called the Breymann Redoubt. With Arnold in command, the Americans captured the temporary fortification, forcing the main British army to fall back to Saratoga. During the fighting, Arnold was wounded when his leg was crushed under the weight of his dying horse.

Benedict Arnold was a hero at Saratoga, only to betray his country later by aiding the British.

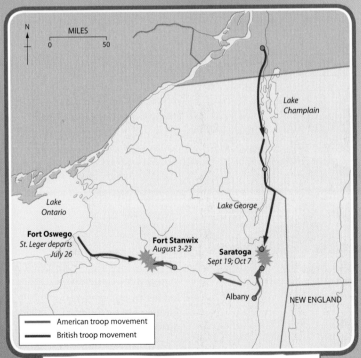

This map shows the ill-fated plan by the British to cut New England off from the rest of the colonies.

Overwhelming Force

On September 19, the Americans stopped Burgoyne's advance approximately 10 miles below Saratoga, New York. During the first Battle of Saratoga, also called the Battle of Freeman's Farm, Burgoyne suffered 560 casualties, nearly twice as many as the Americans.

When the smoke cleared, U.S. General Horatio Gates positioned his army between Burgoyne's forces and Albany. On October 7, with supplies running low, Burgoyne tried to break free, but the Americans attacked, overwhelming the redcoats. Burgoyne was forced to retreat north to Saratoga. The Americans followed and surrounded the British. With nowhere to turn, Burgoyne surrendered on October 17. The victory at Saratoga convinced France to enter the war on the side of the Americans, helping to keep the revolution alive.

Battle of New Orleans

By 1812, it had been more than 30 years since the American rebels fought the British for freedom. President James Madison had to decide whether to ask Congress for the United States to declare war against Great Britain again.

The British were restricting America's overseas trade. They were seizing U.S. ships and forcing American sailors into the British navy. President Madison was faced with defending America's honor and its people. He asked Congress for, and received, permission to go to war. Disaster soon followed.

During the War of 1812, British soldiers returned to fight again on American soil. American goods, which were to be exported to other countries, rotted on the wharves of American ports. The U.S. government was unable to pay its bills. The New England states discussed **seceding** and making a separate peace with Britain. In 1814, the British captured and burned the U.S. Capitol and White House.

Battle Lines

Conflict
War of 1812 (1812–1815)

Dates of Battle
January 8, 1815

Principal American Commander
General Andrew Jackson

General Andrew Jackson led his troops at the Battle of New Orleans during the War of 1812.

Jackson Takes Charge

This was the state of affairs in December 1814, when American General Andrew Jackson arrived in New Orleans, Louisiana. The British wanted to seize the strategic city, which is located at the mouth of the Mississippi River. The river served as a major trade route to other countries, and the British wanted to control the waterway. The people of New Orleans were in a panic. British troops were only 9 miles away. With an American force of about 6,000 troops, mostly made up of militia and slaves, Jackson rushed to the city's defense. He ordered the building of **parapets** made of wood, earth, and cotton bales. Early on January 8, 1815, the fight for New Orleans began.

Just the Facts

A poem entitled "In Defense of Fort McHenry," written during the War of 1812 by Francis Scott Key, was the original name of "The Star-Spangled Banner," which later became the national anthem of the United States.

Quick Fight

The British stormed the American defenses in a thick fog. As the fog lifted, the Americans had a clear target for their guns. Cannons quickly tore huge gaps in the British lines, killing many senior officers. The British became mired in the swamps around the city. A handful of British soldiers made it up to the top of the parapets, only to be killed or captured.

The battle ended with an American victory. The war was finished by the time the battle was fought. News of a peace treaty, signed in Belgium, arrived in Washington, D.C., at the same time as news of Jackson's victory. The fighting lasted only 30 minutes. Yet, it had long-lasting effects. The Battle of New Orleans made Jackson a national hero and propelled him to the U.S. presidency in 1829. The battle, along with the war itself, increased American self-confidence and **nationalism**.

Before the British attacked Jackson and his troops, the Americans built an earthen fortification on the banks of a narrow, dry canal between the British camp and New Orleans.

Battle of Veracruz ④

The United States was coming of age in the 1840s. It was a time for the country to stretch its legs.

Some Americans believed it was the "manifest destiny" of the United States to expand its borders on the continent. They set their sights on winning new territory, especially Texas, from Mexico.

General Winfield Scott led the U.S. attack on Veracruz during the Mexican-American War.

Battle Lines

Conflict
Mexican-American War (1846–1848)

Dates of Battle
March 1847

Principal American Commanders
General Winfield Scott and Commodore David Conner

Battle for Texas

In 1845, the U.S. **annexed** Texas, making it an American territory. A year later, Mexico and the United States went to war. The Americans quickly routed the Mexicans in every battle. In Washington, D.C., President James K. Polk decided the fastest victory would be achieved by capturing Mexico City. Taking the port of Veracruz on the Gulf of Mexico was vital to that mission. A massive fort with more than 120 guns protected the walled city. U.S. General Winfield Scott and Commodore David Conner determined that the best way to take Veracruz was to land the army on a beach about 3 miles south of the city.

Storming the Shore

On March 9, about 10,000 U.S. troops swept ashore in specially designed boats, the first amphibious landing in U.S. military history. Meeting little resistance, Scott's men marched inland, surrounding the city and its garrison of 3,000 Mexican troops.

The Americans laid **siege** to the city. Engineers dug trenches that slowly encircled Veracruz. No one could get in or out. On March 22, heavy guns pummeled Veracruz and its fortifications. On March 28, the Mexican forces surrendered.

Veracruz was a critical U.S. victory. It paved the way for Scott's march to Mexico City and ultimate victory. When Mexico surrendered, the United States had captured more than 500,000 square miles of territory from Texas to California. The war opened up new territories for the United States. Unfortunately, it also allowed the expansion of slavery, which would spark a civil war 13 years later.

Many soldiers who fought alongside each other during the Mexican-American War, including Robert E. Lee and Ulysses S. Grant, would become enemies during the U.S. Civil War.

Remembering the Alamo

First built as a mission in 1718, the Alamo was one of several Spanish settlements along the San Antonio River in Texas. In the 1820s, when Mexico declared its independence from Spain, many American families moved to Texas. The Mexican government passed strict laws aimed at the Texans. In December 1835, the Texans occupied the Alamo. They declared themselves independent and formed the short-lived Lone Star Republic. From February 23 to March 6, 1836, Mexican troops stormed the mission. The outnumbered Americans fought valiantly in the battle but were defeated.

A total of 189 Texans fortified the Alamo during the siege. None survived the battle.

Battle of Gettysburg ⑤

The Civil War was the bloodiest conflict in American history. The Confederacy, made up of the southern states, fought against the Union, or northern states. The war was two years old when Confederate General Robert E. Lee decided to march his army into the northern state of Pennsylvania.

Lee hoped a successful invasion of the North would turn public opinion against the war and force President Abraham Lincoln to seek peace. The Confederates wanted to form their own country. "We should assume the aggressive," Lee said.

Robert E. Lee's Army of Northern Virginia needed a victory in Pennsylvania if the Confederacy was to survive.

Battle Lines

Conflict
U.S. Civil War (1861–1865)

Dates of Battle
July 1–3, 1863

Principal Commanders
General George Meade (Federal Army)
General Robert E. Lee (Confederate Army)

Gettysburg: Day 1

On July 1, 1863, rumors filled the Confederate ranks that there were shoes in the small town of Gettysburg. The rebels needed shoes badly. As the rebels converged on Gettysburg from the north, Union **cavalry** spotted the enemy advance about 3 miles from the town. After a day-long battle, the rebels chased the Union soldiers through the streets.

Union General Winfield Scott Hancock rallied the retreating men. He ordered them to form defensive positions on nearby Culp's Hill and Cemetery Hill. Lee ordered Confederate General Richard Ewell to attack the Federals before nightfall if possible, but Ewell did not. Although the Confederates had won the day, Union forces were able to fortify the high ground south of town.

The Federal front line resembled a fishhook. The curve of the hook ran along Culp's Hill and Cemetery Hill on the right. The shank, or shaft of the hook, was to the left. It ran down Cemetery Ridge all the way to two hills called Big and Little Round Top. "I cannot sleep," Gettysburg resident Sarah Broadhead wrote that night. "We know not what the morrow will bring forth."

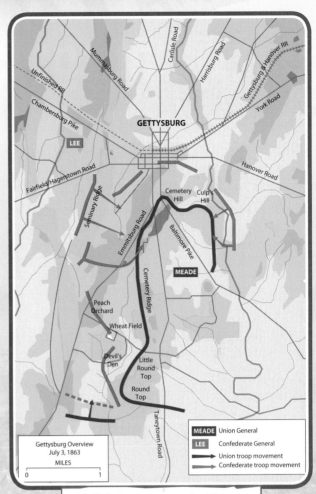

The fighting between the Union and Confederate armies took place not only in the village of Gettysburg, but also along several key positions along the battlefront.

Gettysburg: Days 2 and 3

When the sun rose on July 2, approximately 65,000 Confederates and 85,000 Union troops faced one another. Although Confederate General James Longstreet urged Lee to fight the Union elsewhere, Lee was determined to engage the Union. He wanted the Federal forces off the high ground. Union General George Meade would not make it easy.

The Battle of Gettysburg was a major defeat for the Confederacy. However, the war would last another two years.

Lee and Meade fought over several important spots on the second day of battle, including the Peach Orchard, Devil's Den, Cemetery Hill, and the Wheat Field. Each skirmish was a mini battle. Some of the most intense fighting took place on Little Round Top, a nub of a hill at the end of the Federal lines. Lee wanted his men to capture the summit and train their cannons on the Federal line, smashing it to pieces.

The task fell to a group of Alabama soldiers. They charged up Little Round Top several times, hoping to dislodge the Federals. Each time, they were beaten back. With their ammunition running low, Union Colonel Joshua Chamberlain, from Maine, ordered his men to fix bayonets and plunge down the hillside as the rebels charged. The attack surprised the rebels, who retreated down the hill. At the end of the day, the Federal lines on Cemetery Ridge held.

Union General George Meade outfought and outmaneuvered the seemingly invincible Robert E. Lee.

In the End

On July 3, the third day of battle, Lee tried to break through the center of the Federal defense on Cemetery Ridge. About 15,000 Confederates under the command of General George Pickett marched directly into Union cannon and rifle fire. The charge failed. Lee and his men had lost the battle. They limped home to Virginia. "It was my entire fault," Lee said.

Over the three-day battle, about 51,000 troops were killed, wounded, or went missing. Gettysburg was the bloodiest battle of the war. Had the Confederates won, they might have marched on to Washington, D.C., forcing Lincoln to seek peace. Instead, it would be the last time the Confederacy would threaten the North on its own soil.

In 1898, many Americans would have been hard pressed to find Cuba on a map.

As spring turned to summer, the United States found itself at war with Spain in Cuba. Spain was the European nation that controlled the Caribbean island. Some Americans wanted to help Cuba become an independent nation. Others cared less about Cuban freedom and more about making the United States a colonial power, just like Spain.

Battle Lines

Conflict
Spanish-American War
(April 25–August 13, 1898)

Dates of Battle
May 1, 1898

Principal American Commander
Commodore George Dewey

William Randolph Hearst heard from Frederic Remington, who had been sent to Cuba as war correspondent and artist, that all was quiet on that island. Hearst supposedly replied, "You supply the pictures, and I'll supply the war."

Read All About It

U.S. newspaper publisher William Randolph Hearst and his rival, Joseph Pulitzer, were two important people who wanted the United States to become involved in Cuba. They supported the war, and not only for political reasons. Writing about the war increased the number of newspapers they sold.

Both men used their publications to whip the nation into a frenzy. They published horrific stories and drawings depicting the real, or imagined, atrocities suffered by the Cubans at the hands of the Spanish. The United States sent the battleship USS *Maine* to Havana Harbor, as a precaution. When the ship exploded, the American public assumed it had been attacked by Spain and demanded revenge.

Just the Facts

The term "yellow journalism," used to describe the sensational news coverage practiced by newspapers in the 1890s, came from a comic called "Hogan's Alley." The comic featured a character named "the yellow kid."

Planning for Battle

The U.S. declared war on April 25. The first battle took place in the faraway Philippines, a Spanish colony in the Pacific. For several years, the United States had been preparing for a war with Spain. Part of the American strategy was to strike the Philippines.

On February 25, Assistant Secretary of the U.S. Navy Theodore Roosevelt had ordered Commodore George Dewey and the Asiatic Squadron to prepare for battle. Roosevelt was one of many U.S. officials pushing President William McKinley to fight the Spanish. On April 25, Dewey set sail. As the squadron raced toward Manila, the Spanish prepared their defenses. They mined the bay's main channel, only to find the water was too deep and the entrance too wide for the mines to be effective.

New Colonial Power

Finally, on May 1, under the cover of darkness, Dewey's fleet slipped into Manila Bay. When dawn broke, the Americans quickly overpowered the Spanish fleet. The press reported that the battle was so one-sided that Dewey ordered his men to take a break and eat a light meal in the middle of the fighting.

Dewey's victory was so complete that McKinley sent more than 10,000 soldiers to capture Manila. Because of Dewey's victory, the U.S. took control of the Philippines and became a major power in the Pacific.

Theodore Roosevelt was a hero during the Spanish-American War and went on to become the president of the United States.

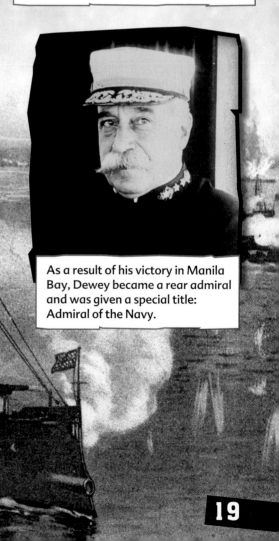

As a result of his victory in Manila Bay, Dewey became a rear admiral and was given a special title: Admiral of the Navy.

Only one U.S. sailor died during battle, and that was due to heat exhaustion. The Spanish, however, were not as lucky. Hundreds died.

Second Battle of the Marne

By the time the United States entered World War I in 1917, hundreds of thousands of Europeans had already died in the war.

Many Americans did not want the U.S. involved in a foreign war. But U.S. ties with France and Great Britain, who were battling Germany and its allies in Europe, were strong. By 1917, tensions between the U.S. and Germany were running high, as German submarines attacked merchant ships in the Atlantic Ocean.

Finally, Congress declared war on April 6. The U.S. quickly mobilized the American Expeditionary Force (AEF) under General John J. Pershing. The first U.S. troops of the AEF reached France in June 1917.

Battle Lines

Conflict
World War I (1914–1918)

Dates of Battle
July 15–August 5, 1918

Principal American Commander
John J. Pershing

Divide and Conquer

On March 21, 1918, the Germans launched a huge spring offensive, hoping to win the war. Over the next four months, the Germans won several key battles. Believing victory was near, German General Erich Ludendorff devised a plan to draw Allied forces to the Marne River and away from the front lines in Flanders, Belgium. Once the Allies split their forces, Ludendorff planned to attack the weakened positions in Flanders and march to victory.

The German attack at the Marne began on July 15. After unleashing a massive artillery bombardment, German troops advanced on the French trenches, only to find no one there. "Our guns bombarded empty trenches; our gas-shells gassed empty artillery positions," wrote one German officer.

At the Marne, many U.S. gunners used machine guns, which were developed and improved during World War I.

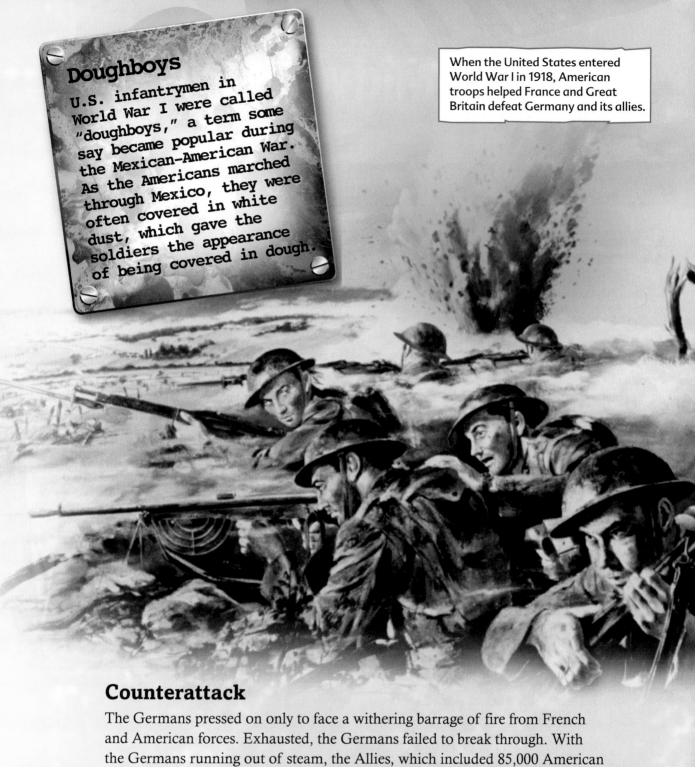

Doughboys

U.S. infantrymen in World War I were called "doughboys," a term some say became popular during the Mexican-American War. As the Americans marched through Mexico, they were often covered in white dust, which gave the soldiers the appearance of being covered in dough.

When the United States entered World War I in 1918, American troops helped France and Great Britain defeat Germany and its allies.

Counterattack

The Germans pressed on only to face a withering barrage of fire from French and American forces. Exhausted, the Germans failed to break through. With the Germans running out of steam, the Allies, which included 85,000 American soldiers, launched a counterattack.

On July 18, thousands of Allied troops supported by hundreds of tanks, airplanes, and artillery moved against the Germans. By July 20, the Germans withdrew, and by the beginning of August were back to where they started in March. The Allied victory at the Marne in 1918 was Germany's last large-scale attempt to win the war. In November, Germany surrendered.

Battle of Midway (8)

By 1941, Japan had expanded its empire in South Asia. On December 7, 1941, the Japanese launched a surprise attack on the American naval base at Pearl Harbor, Hawaii.

The United States, which had hoped to stay out of World War II, was now in the thick of it. During the early months of the war, the Japanese sliced through the Pacific, capturing the Philippines, Guam, parts of New Guinea, and the Solomon Islands.

Gateway to America

Hoping to continue their winning streak, Japanese Admiral Isoroku Yamamoto, who had planned the sneak attack on Pearl Harbor, now eyed the tiny island of Midway. Located about 1,000 miles from Hawaii, Midway was the gateway to Hawaii and the West Coast of the United States. Yamamoto wanted to establish a base on Midway, hoping to draw out and annihilate America's remaining aircraft carriers.

Yamamoto needed to fool the Americans before capturing Midway. He sent a small task force to attack the Aleutian Islands off Alaska as a **diversion**, hoping to lure the main American force away from the Japanese battle fleet steaming toward Midway.

Battle Lines

Conflict
World War II (1939–1945)

Dates of Battle
June 1942

Principal American Commander
Admiral Chester W. Nimitz

Among the U.S. targets at the Battle of Midway were Japan's heavy cruisers. About 3,500 Japanese lost their lives.

Ambush

The Americans discovered Yamamoto's secret plan. In response, U.S. Admiral Chester Nimitz decided to ambush the Japanese, so forces from both sides converged on the island. On June 4, 1942, a Japanese scout plane spotted the U.S. carriers approaching Midway. That morning an air battle began. American dive bombers attacked the Japanese carriers *Akagi*, *Soryu*, and *Kaga*. The *Akagi* exploded in a massive firestorm as American planes dropped bombs on its deck. The other Japanese carriers burst into flames.

Although the Japanese sank the U.S. carrier *Yorktown*, Yamamoto was badly beaten. His task force limped back to Japan. Japan's loss at Midway was a turning point in the war in the Pacific. The Japanese navy would never recover. The momentum in the Pacific war had now swung to the U.S.

The Japanese lost four aircraft carriers and 270 aircraft in the Battle of Midway.

Japanese Admiral Isoroku Yamamoto thought his attack on Pearl Harbor would make the United States anxious for peace. Instead, it brought the country into the war.

First Nuclear Superpower

The United States is the only nation to have used an atomic weapon in battle. The U.S. dropped two nuclear bombs on Japan in 1945, which marked the end of the war in the Pacific. One was dropped on the city of Hiroshima, the other on Nagasaki.

Battle of Chosin Reservoir

Although World War II ended with a U.S. and Allied victory, a new kind of war began afterward, the Cold War.

Cold War in Korea

The Cold War was an ideological struggle between **communism** and democracy. The Soviet Union, China, and other communist nations lined up against the United States and its democratic allies. The Cold War erupted when, on June 25, 1950, communist soldiers from North Korea invaded South Korea. The South Korean army retreated in a panic. Fearing a communist takeover of the South, the United Nations (U.N.), led by the United States, stepped in.

At first, the North Koreans nearly pushed U.N. forces into the sea. But the U.N. regrouped and chased the enemy back to North Korea. U.S. General Douglas MacArthur was in charge of U.N. forces. At the end of November, he launched a counter-offensive along the Yalu River.

Battle Lines

Conflict
Korean War (1950–1953)

Dates of Battle
November 26–December 13, 1950

Principal American Commander
Gen. Douglas MacArthur

General Douglas MacArthur made the biggest mistake of his military career when he launched an attack near the Chinese border during the Korean War.

CHANGJIN (CHOSIN) RESERVOIR

Chinese Army

Chinese Army

Line of U.N. Retreat

MILES

0   10

This map shows the line of retreat of U.N. forces during the Battle of Chosin.

The Chinese Attack

It was a terrible mistake. Just as the U.N. counter-offensive began, more than 200,000 communist Chinese troops poured across the river on the side of the North Koreans. MacArthur was shaken. "We face an entirely new war," he said.

The Chinese and United Nations faced off at the Chosin Reservoir. On November 26, about 120,000 Chinese soldiers surrounded U.N. forces at Chosin, including the American 1st Marine Division. The chances of escape were slim. In addition to facing numerous attacks from the Chinese, the Americans had to deal with below-zero temperatures.

When Chinese troops crossed the Yalu River into North Korea, it changed the nature of the Korean War.

Road of Escape

For three bloody days, the Americans successfully defended their positions. They then began to fight their way out. The only avenue of escape was Toktong Pass, a snake-like road that twisted and turned between steep hills. The Marines controlled the road, but if the Chinese captured a critical section of it, the escape route for 8,000 Marines would be blocked.

As the U.S. Marines withdrew from Chosin, the cold was so intense that the uncovered faces of soldiers suffered frostbite.

For five days and five nights, a lone company of Marines, called Fox Company, defended that section of roadway, keeping the door open for the Americans to escape. Although they lost the battle, U.N. troops had inflicted heavy casualties on the Chinese. Historians estimate that 25,000 to more than 37,000 Chinese troops died or were wounded.

Battle of Hue (10)

Vietnam was a colony of France before World War II, when the Japanese conquered the region. With Japan's defeat, Vietnamese leader Ho Chi Minh and his communist followers, called the Viet Minh, sought an independent Vietnam. Their struggle led to the Vietnam War, one of the most controversial wars in American history.

U.S. Enters the Mix

The French took control of Vietnam again after Japan lost the war. Hoping to free Vietnam from French rule, Ho and his supporters fought and defeated the French in a **guerrilla** war. But Vietnam did not gain its independence with victory. Instead, the United States and its U.N. allies stepped in.

In 1954, diplomats split Vietnam in half. Communists ruled the North, while non-communists ruled the South. Eventually, the Viet Minh decided that war was the only way to fight for and unify the country. By 1964, American troops were fighting communist supporters from the South, known as the Viet Cong.

Battle Lines

Conflict
Vietnam War (1964–1975)

Dates of Battle
January–February, 1968

Principal American Commander
General Foster LaHue

The Viet Cong were loosely organized at first, but by the time they fought at Hue, they were experts at guerrilla fighting.

Tet Offensive

A pivotal battle of the Vietnam War occurred in 1968 along the Perfume River in South Vietnam. In January 1968, communist forces launched a major attack in Hue (pronounced "way"). Hue was a holy place of ancient Buddhist temples and palaces. The communists attacked during the most important holiday in Vietnam, the celebration of the lunar new year, known as Tet. During the Tet Offensive, the communists struck many cities and military bases at the same time.

On the morning of January 31, the communists moved on Hue from three directions. They met little resistance from the South Vietnamese. After seizing the center of town, the communists killed their enemies in house-to-house fighting.

The most intense fighting during the Battle of Hue occurred near the Citadel, located in the heart of the city.

Hue: The Fight Continues

U.S. Marines were called in from an air base to the south. American helicopters entered the city from the north. The Marines moved toward the Citadel, a walled section of the city near the Imperial Palace, dodging sniper fire and **booby traps**. The Marines, who were accustomed to fighting in jungles, were not prepared to fight inside a city, but they adapted.

At first, the Americans did not shell the city with artillery or bomb it from the air because of its historical significance. As the fighting grew more intense, the ban was lifted, but poor weather conditions hampered the progress of the American fighter planes. For 10 days, the battle raged.

Intense sniper fire rained on U.S. troops during the Battle of Hue.

The Citadel

Finally, the Americans and South Vietnamese fought their way to the Citadel. The communists had raised their flag high above the Citadel's walls. On February 24, South Vietnamese troops, many of whom grew up in Hue, ripped the flag down. Five days later, the Americans and South Vietnamese captured the Imperial Palace.

Public Opinion

About 50 U.S. Marines were killed during the battle, along with about 400 South Vietnamese soldiers. An estimated 5,000 communist soldiers lost their lives. Thousands of South Vietnamese and others were massacred by the Viet Cong. Although the Battle of Hue was considered a U.S. victory, American public opinion turned against the war.

Just the Facts

The Vietnam War claimed 58,000 American lives. It is often considered the first war the United States did not win.

Hue was built like two separate cities on both sides of the Perfume River, so capturing its bridges was important.

War-Torn World

In recent decades, the United States has found itself under attack for the first time since Pearl Harbor. America has fought in far-off countries where U.S. interests have been challenged. Here are a few of the key battles:

The Battle of Khafji
(Persian Gulf War, 1991)

In August 1990, Iraq's dictator Saddam Hussein invaded Kuwait to take over its vast oil fields. Five months later, the U.S. led a coalition of nations to intervene.

On January 29, 1991, Iraqi tanks stormed into Saudi Arabia from Kuwait, attacking the coastal city of Khafji from three different directions. It was a major offensive launched by Saddam involving three of his best-mechanized divisions. U.S. forces quickly turned back most of the attacks, while a single Iraqi column occupied the city for one night. Aided by U.S. artillery and aircraft, Saudi troops took back the city. U.S. and coalition forces soon drove back the Iraqi forces to their own borders.

Two Afghan fighters armed with an old Soviet rifle and radio receivers kept a watchful eye for the Taliban and supporters of Osama bin Laden in Tora Bora.

A U.S. tank fired its main gun into a building during a firefight in Fallujah, Iraq.

Battle of Tora Bora
(Afghanistan, December 12–17, 2001)

In October 2001, one month after terrorists attacked the World Trade Center and Pentagon on September 11, American troops invaded Afghanistan. Their plan was to destroy the terrorist bases and topple the ruling Taliban government. At the time, the mastermind of the 9/11 attacks, Osama bin Laden, was hiding in the Tora Bora region of Afghanistan, near Pakistan's border.

U.S. Army Rangers in the region were out-numbered and were ordered not to engage until they could be reinforced. Afghanistan's militia was asked to go after bin Laden. By the time the battle between the Afghans and terrorists was over, bin Laden had escaped on horseback. The U.S. came under criticism because it did not lead the attack and instead relied on the poorly trained Afghans.

Second Battle of Fallujah
(Iraq War, November 7–December 23, 2004)

In 2003, the U.S. and its allies invaded Iraq to overthrow Saddam Hussein. Although the mission successfully ousted Hussein, the Iraq War took an unexpected turn when terrorists and local militias, known as insurgents, began fighting the Americans.

In the spring of 2004, the U.S. Marines captured the Iraqi city of Fallujah from the insurgents. The Marines left a group of local men to guard the city. By November, the insurgents retook Fallujah and its stockpiled weapons. On November 7, the Americans attacked Fallujah for a second time. Using tanks and infantry, the Americans pushed deep into the city and overwhelmed the insurgents. On November 16, U.S. commanders announced the city was secure, though the battle did not officially end until December 23.

Glossary

allies—partners in war

annexed—incorporated legally into another country or state

booby traps—secretly hidden devices to kill or injure the enemy

cavalry—soldiers on horseback

communism—a social and economic system characterized by a classless society and the absence of private property

diversion—a mock attack aimed at drawing the enemy away from the intended main attack

fascism—a political ideology in which the state, often controlled by a dictator, controls most aspects of life

guerrilla—of or about a resistance movement; a soldier or member of a resistance movement

nationalism—a devotion to one's nation; patriotism

parapets—low, protective fortifications along the edge of a military trench

reinforce—strengthen or support with additional troops

seceding—breaking away and forming a separate country

siege—the surrounding of a town or military base by an opposing army that wants to capture it

Index